Verbatim Transcript of Combatant Status Review Tribunal Hearing for ISN 10024

OPENING

REPORTER: On the record

RECORDER: All rise.

PRESIDENT: Remain seated and come to order. Go ahead, Recorder.

RECORDER: This Tribunal is being conducted at 1328 March 10, 2007 on board U.S. Naval Base Guantanamo Bay, Cuba. The following personnel are present:
Captain [REDACTED], United States Navy, President
Lieutenant Colonel [REDACTED], United States Air Force, Member
Lieutenant Colonel [REDACTED], United States Marine Corps, Member
Lieutenant Colonel [REDACTED], United States Air Force, Personal Representative
Language Analysis [REDACTED]
Gunnery Sergeant [REDACTED], United States Marine Corps, Reporter
Lieutenant Colonel [REDACTED], United States Army, Recorder
Captain [REDACTED] is the Judge Advocate member of the Tribunal.

OATH SESSION 1

RECORDER: All Rise.

PRESIDENT: The Recorder will be sworn. Do you, Lieutenant Colonel [REDACTED] solemnly swear that you will faithfully perform the duties as Recorder assigned in this Tribunal so help you God?

RECORDER: I do.

PRESIDENT: The Reporter will now be sworn. The Recorder will administer the oath.

RECORDER: Do you Gunnery Sergeant [DELETED] swear or affirm that you will faithfully discharge your duties as Reporter assigned in this Tribunal so help you God?

REPORTER: I do.

PRESIDENT: The Translator will be sworn.

RECORDER: Do you swear or affirm that you will faithfully perform the duties of Translator in the case now in hearing so help you God?

TRANSLATOR: I do.

PRESIDENT: We will take a brief recess now in order in to bring Detainee into the room. Recorder note the date and time.

RECORDER: The time is 1:30 pm hours on 10 March 2007. This Tribunal is in now in recess. [The Tribunal recessed at 1330, 10 March 2007. The members withdrew from the hearing room.]

CONVENING AUTHORITY

RECORDER: All Rise. [The Tribunal reconvened and the members entered the room at 1334, 10 March 2007.]

PRESIDENT: This hearing will come to order. Please be seated.

PRESIDENT: Before we begin, Khalid Sheikh Muhammad, I understand you speak and understand English. Is that correct?

DETAINEE: [Detainee nods his head in affirmative].

PRESIDENT: Alright. Are you comfortable in continuing in English or would you like everything translated in Arabic?

DETAINEE: Everything in English but if I have a problem the linguist will help me.

PRESIDENT: We will proceed in English. If you indicate to me that you would like something translated we will go ahead and do that. Alright?

PRESIDENT: This Tribunal is convened by order of the Director, Combatant Status Review Tribunals under the provisions of his Order of 22 February 2007.

PRESIDENT: This Tribunal will determine whether Khalid Sheikh Muhammad meets the criteria to be designated as an enemy combatant against the United States or its coalition partners or otherwise meets the criteria to be designated as an enemy combatant.

OATH SESSION 2

PRESIDENT: The members of this Tribunal shall now be sworn. All rise.

RECORDER: Do you swear or affirm that you will faithfully perform your duties as a member of this Tribunal; that you will impartially examine and inquire into the matter now before you according to your conscience, and the laws and regulations provided; that you will make such findings of fact and conclusions as are supported by the evidence presented; that in determining those facts, you will use your professional knowledge, best judgment, and common sense; and that you will make such findings as are appropriate according to the best of your understanding of the rules, regulations, and laws governing this proceeding, and guided by your concept of justice so help you God?

TRIBUNAL: I do.

PRESIDENT: The Recorder will now administer the oath to the Personal Representative.

RECORDER: Do you swear or affirm that you will faithfully perform the duties of Personal Representative in this Tribunal so help you God?

PERSONAL
REPRESENTATIVE: I do.

PRESIDENT: Please be seated.

PRESIDENT: The Recorder, Reporter, and Translator have previously been sworn.

EXPLANATION OF PROCEEDINGS

PRESIDENT: Khalid Sheikh Muhammad, you are hereby advised that the following applies during this hearing:

PRESIDENT: You may be present at all open sessions of the Tribunal. However, if you become disorderly, you will be removed from the hearing, and the Tribunal will continue to hear evidence in your absence.

PRESIDENT: You may not be compelled to testify at this Tribunal. However, you may testify if you wish to do so. Your testimony can be under oath or unsworn.

PRESIDENT: You may have the assistance of a Personal Representative at the hearing. Your assigned Personal Representative is present.

PRESIDENT: You may present evidence to this Tribunal, including the testimony of witnesses who are reasonably available and whose testimony is relevant to this hearing. You may question witnesses testifying at the Tribunal.

PRESIDENT: You may examine documents or statements offered into evidence other than classified information. However, certain documents may be partially masked for security reasons.

PRESIDENT: Khalid Sheikh Muhammad, do you understand this process?

DETAINEE: Yes. If I have question can I ask you?

PRESIDENT: Yes, you may.

DETAINEE: About the testimony which I ask about the witnesses.

PRESIDENT: Yes, I'm going to address the witnesses shortly. So, if you will bear with us I will take that up in a few moments.

DETAINEE: Okay.

PRESIDENT: Do you have any questions concerning the Tribunal process?

DETAINEE: Okay by me.

PRESENTATION OF UNCLASSIFIED INFORMATION

PRESIDENT: Personal Representative, please provide the Tribunal with the Detainee Election Form.

PERSONAL
REPRESENTATIVE: I am handing the Tribunal the Detainee Election Form, which was previously marked as Exhibit D-a.

PRESIDENT: Alright, the Tribunal has received Exhibit D-a that indicates the Detainee wants to participate in the Tribunal and wants the assistance of the Personal Representative.

RECORDER PRESENTS UNCLASSIFIED

PRESIDENT: Recorder, please provide the Tribunal with the unclassified evidence.

RECORDER: I am handing the Tribunal what has previously been marked as Exhibit R-1, the unclassified summary of the evidence that relates to this Detainee's status as an enemy combatant. A translated copy of this exhibit was provided to the Personal

ISN #10024
Enclosure (3)
Page 4 of 26

Representative in advance of this hearing for presentation to the Detainee. In addition, I am handing to the Tribunal the following unclassified exhibits, marked as Exhibit R-2. Copies of these Exhibits have previously been provided to the Personal Representative. [Documents presented to Tribunal]

PRESIDENT: Recorder, please read the unclassified summary of evidence for the record. But before you proceed, Khalid Sheikh Muhammad, let me remind you that you must not comment on this evidence at this time. You will be provided with an opportunity shortly to provide any comments that you would like. Recorder, please proceed.

RECORDER: The following facts support the determination that the Detainee is an enemy combatant:

Paragraph a. On the morning of 11 September 2001, four airliners traveling over the United States were hijacked. The flights hijacked were: American Airlines Flight 11, United Airlines Flight 175, American Airlines Flight 77, and United Airlines Flight 93. At approximately 8:46 a.m., American Airlines Flight 11 crashed into the North Tower of the World Trade Center, resulting in the collapse of the tower at approximately 10:25 a.m. At approximately 9:05 a.m., United Airlines Flight 175 crashed into the South Tower of the World Trade Center, resulting in the collapse of the tower at approximately 9:55 a.m. At approximately 9:37 a.m., American Airlines Flight 77 crashed into the southwest side of the Pentagon in Arlington, Virginia. At approximately 10:03 a.m., United Airlines Flight 93 crashed in Stoney Creek Township, Pennsylvania. These crashes and subsequent damage to the World Trade Center and the Pentagon resulted in the deaths of 2,972 persons in New York, Virginia, and Pennsylvania.

Paragraph b. The Detainee served as the head of the al Qaida military committee and was Usama bin Laden's principal al Qaida operative who directed the 11 September 2001 attacks in the United States.

Paragraph c. In an interview with an al Jazeera reporter in June 2002, the Detainee stated he was the head of the al Qaida military committee.

Paragraph d. A computer hard drive seized during the capture of the Detainee contained information about the four airplanes hijacked on 11 September 2001 including code names, airline company, flight number, target, pilot name and background information, and names of the hijackers.

Paragraph e. A computer hard drive seized during the capture of the Detainee contained photographs of 19 individuals identified as the 11 September 2001 hijackers.

Paragraph f. A computer hard drive seized during the capture of the Detainee contained a document that listed the pilot license fees for Mohammad Atta and biographies for some of the 11 September 2001 hijackers.

Paragraph g. A computer hard drive seized during the capture of the Detainee contained images of passports and an image of Mohammad Atta.

Paragraph h. A computer hard drive seized during the capture of the Detainee contained transcripts of chat sessions belonging to at least one of the 11 September 2001 hijackers.

Paragraph i. The Detainee directed an individual to travel to the United States to case targets for a second wave of attacks.

Paragraph j. A computer hard drive seized during the capture of the Detainee contained three letters from Usama bin Laden.

Paragraph k. A computer hard drive seized during the capture of the Detainee contained spreadsheets that describe money assistance to families of known al Qaida members.

Paragraph l. The Detainee's name was on a list in a computer seized in connection with a threat to United States airlines, United States embassies and the Pope.

Paragraph m. The Detainee wrote the *bojinka plot*, the airline bomb plot which was later found on his nephew Ramzi Yousef's computer.

Paragraph n. The *bojinka plot* is also known as the Manila air investigation.

Paragraph o. The Manila air investigation uncovered the Detainee conspired with others to plant explosive devices aboard American jetliners while those aircraft were scheduled to be airborne and loaded with passengers on their way to the United States.

Paragraph p. The Detainee was in charge of and funded an attack against United States military vessels heading to the port of Djibouti.

Paragraph q. A computer hard drive seized during the capture of the Detainee contained a letter to the United Arab Emirates threatening attack if their government continued to help the United States.

Paragraph r. During the capture of the Detainee, information used exclusively by al Qaida operational managers to communicate with operatives was found.

Paragraph s. The Detainee received funds from Kuwaiti-based Islamic extremist groups and delivered the funds to al Qaida members.

Paragraph t. A computer hard drive seized during the capture of the Detainee contained a document that summarized operational procedures and training requirements of an al Qaida cell.

Paragraph u. A computer hard drive seized during the capture of the Detainee contained a list of killed and wounded al Qaida martyrs.

And lastly, Paragraph v. Passport photographs of al Qaida operatives were seized during the capture of the Detainee.

RECORDER: Sir, this concludes the summary of unclassified evidence.

PRESIDENT: Very well.

PRESIDENT: Personal Representative, does the Detainee have any evidence to present to this Tribunal?

PERSONAL
REPRESENTATIVE: Yes, sir. I am handing to the Tribunal the following unclassified exhibits marked as Exhibits D-b through D-d. Copies of these exhibits have been previously provided to the Recorder. [Documents presented to Tribunal]

PRESIDENT: Exhibit D-b appears to be a statement that the Detainee has provided.

PERSONAL
REPRESENTATIVE: Yes, Sir.

PRESIDENT: Alright. And Exhibit D-c contains hand written notes that appear to be Arabic and English as well as the typed version of that. Is that correct?

PERSONAL
REPRESENTATIVE: Yes, Sir.

PRESIDENT: Alright. And D-d is a written statement regarding alleged abuse or treatment that the Detainee received.

PERSONAL
REPRESENTATIVE: Yes, Sir.

PRESIDENT: Alright. We will go into those shortly.

PRESIDENT: Khalid Sheikh Muhammad, you may now make an oral statement to the Tribunal, and you have the assistance of your Personal Representative in doing so. Do you wish to make an oral statement to this Tribunal?

DETAINEE: He will start, the Personal Representative; PR will read then later I will comment.

PRESIDENT: Very well, you may proceed.

RECORDER: Sir, would you hold one moment?

PRESIDENT: Yes.

RECORDER: Ah, before the Detainee makes a statement, ah, I'd like to ah.

PRESIDENT: Question of the oath?

RECORDER: Ah, no sir.

RECORDER: Concerning classified evidence.

PRESIDENT: Very well.

PRESIDENT: Do you have any further evidence to present at this time, Recorder?

RECORDER: Mr. President, I have no further unclassified evidence for the Tribunal but I respectfully request a closed Tribunal session at an appropriate time to present classified evidence relevant to this Detainee's status as an enemy combatant.

PRESIDENT: Very well, your request for a closed session is granted and will be taken up in due course.

PRESIDENT: You may proceed, PR.

PERSONAL
REPRESENTATIVE: The Detainee responds to the unclassified summary of evidence with the following key points.

PERSONAL
REPRESENTATIVE: "Some paragraphs under paragraph number 3, lead sentence are not related to the context or meaning of the aforementioned lead sentence. For example, paragraph 3-a is only information from news or a historical account of events on 11 September 2001, and note with no specific linkage being made in this

ISN #10024
Enclosure (3)
Page 8 of 26

paragraph to me or the definition of Enemy Combatant. As another example, sub-paragraph 3-n makes no linkage to me or to the definition of Enemy Combatant."

DETAINEE: Are they following along?

PERSONAL
REPRESENTATIVE: Ah, they they have that in front of them for reference.

PRESIDENT: Yes.

DETAINEE: Okay.

PERSONAL
REPRESENTATIVE: Second main point; "There are two false statements in the Summary of Evidence. Sub-paragraph 3-c is false. I never stated to the Al Jazeera reporter that I was the head of the al Qaida military committee. Also, sub-paragraph 3-s is false. I did not receive any funds from Kuwait."

PERSONAL
REPRESENTATIVE: Point number 3. "There is an unfair 'stacking of evidence' in the way the Summary of Evidence is structured. In other words, there are several sub-paragraphs under parent-paragraph 3 which should be combined into one sub-paragraph to avoid creating the false perception that there are more allegations or statements against me specifically than there actually are. For example, sub-paragraphs 3-m through 3-o, which pertain to the *bojinka* plot should be combined into one paragraph, as should paragraphs 3-a through 3-h, which pertain to 9/11."

PERSONAL
REPRESENTATIVE: Lastly, my name is misspelled in the Summary of Evidence. It should be S-h-a-i-k-h or S-h-e-i-k-h, but not S-h-a-y-k-h, as it is in the subject line.

PRESIDENT: Would you like to add anything to that, Khalid Sheikh Muhammad ?

PERSONAL
REPRESENTATIVE: Final statement.

DETAINEE: No, I just want to ask about witnesses.

PRESIDENT: Okay, ah, let's finish with these then I will get to the witnesses.

DETAINEE: Okay.

PRESIDENT: Try to keep it in order.

PRESIDENT: You want to continue, PR? Do you have have another statement?

PERSONAL
REPRESENTATIVE: That concludes this Detainee's response to the, ah, unclassified summary of evidence, sir.

PRESIDENT: Oh.

CALLING OF WITNESSES

PRESIDENT: We will now allow for the calling of witnesses. All witnesses called before this Tribunal may be questioned by the Detainee if present, the Personal Representative, the Recorder, and the Tribunal Members.

PRESIDENT: Does the Recorder have any witnesses to present?

RECORDER: No, sir.

PRESIDENT: Alright.

PRESIDENT: From the Detainee Election Form and I was informed earlier that the Detainee requested the presence of two witnesses to testify here today. Ramzi bin al-Shibh and Mustafa Hawsawi. The Detainee believes the witnesses can provide testimony related to the Detainee's actions specified in the unclassified summary of the evidence.

PRESIDENT: I have had the opportunity to review the request for witnesses and I have made some findings and I'm going to place them on the record now and when I conclude that, Khalid Sheikh Muhammad, you may respond to that if you'd like.

PRESIDENT: First the request for Ramzi bin al-Shib, the proffer of the testimony from the Detainee was that Ramzi is alleged to have been present during the al Jazeera interview in June 2002 during which it is said the Detainee claimed to be head of al Qaida Military Committee. The Detainee claims he never stated that, to be the head of the Military Committee, during the interview and states that Ramzi, if called, can confirm this.

PRESIDENT: This witness is not relevant in the President's view for the following reasons. In the totality of the circumstances and given the nature and quality of the other unclassified evidence, the Detainee's alleged statements as reported in al Jazeera are of limited value and negligible relevancy to the issue of combatant status. As such, any corroboration or contradiction by the proffered witness is not relevant. The creditability determinations with regard to R-2, which is the al Jazeera article, can be made by the Tribunal without the proffered testimony. As such, the Detainee's request for the production of that witness is denied.

PRESIDENT: As to the request for Mustafa Hawsawi, ah, it is proffered that Hawsawi, if called, could testify that the computer/hard drive referenced in the unclassified summary was not this Detainee's property and that the place of the Detainee's capture was not the house of the Detainee. In the President's view this testimony is not relevant to the issues regarding the Detainee's capture or his combatant status for the following reasons.

PRESIDENT: Whether the Detainee had actual legal title or ownership of the computer/hard drive or the house where the capture took place is irrelevant to the determination of the Detainee's status as an enemy combatant. Based on the proffer, if true, Hawsawi's testimony will not provide relevant information. The issue of ownership, while of some interest, is not relevant to status. What is relevant is possession, usage, connection and presence. Hawsawi's testimony will not speak to any relevant information in regard to such points. As such, the request for the production of that witness is denied.

PRESIDENT: If you would like to respond to that, I'll hear you.

DETAINEE: Most of these facts which be written are related to this hard drive. And more than eleven of these facts are related to this computer. Other things are which is very old even nobody can bring any witnesses for that as you written here if it will be ah a value for you for the witness near by you will do it. This computer is not for me. Is for Hawsawi himself. So I'm saying I need Hawsawi because me and him we both been arrested day. Same way. So this computer is from him long time. And also the problem we are not in court and we are not judge and he is not my lawyer but the procedure has been written reported and the way has mostly as certain charged against me; tell him, [Arabic Phrase].

TRANSLATOR: [Translating] They are only accusations.

DETAINEE: So accusations. And the accusations, they are as you put for yourself ah definition for enemy combatant there are also many definitions for that accusation of fact or charges that has been written for any ah. [Arabic Phrase]

TRANSLATOR: [Translating] Person is accused.

ISN #10024
Enclosure (3)
Page 11 of 26

DETAINEE: So, if I been accused then if you want to put facts against me also the definition for these facts. If you now read number N now what is written the *bojinka* plot. Is known many lead investigation it is not related to anything facts to be against me. So when I said computer hard drive/ hard disk, same thing. All these point only one witness he can say yes or not cause he is this computer is under his possession him computer. And also specifically if he said Mohammad Atta picture been this hard drive. I don't think this should accepted. There are many 100 thousand Americans who have a lot of picture on their computer. You cannot say I find Muhammad Atta on your computer then you use this fact against you. Or you find any files in your computer to be what about it's mine, it's not my computer. If this witness, he will state that this known and here that has been ninety percent of what is written is wrong. And for Ramzi, for reporter in Jazeera, he claimed that I state this one and you know the media man. How they are fashionable. What they mean in their own way in a whole different way. They just wrote it so he say I state. But I never stated and I don't have any witnesses and witness are available here at Guantanamo. He is Detainee. He was with me. Which he been mostly in all my interview with him. Me and them, there was three person, me and Ramzi and this reporter. So if you not believe me, not believe him, believe my witness Ramzi. Then he's what he state the reporter most is false. I not denying that I'm not an enemy combatant about this war but I'm denying the report. It not being written in the proper way. Which is really facts and mostly just being gathered many information. General information that form in way of doing, to use in facts against me.

PRESIDENT: I have heard and understood your argument. In order for me to make my determinations regarding the production of witnesses I first have to believe that they are relevant for the reasons that I have stated. For the reasons I have stated, I do not believe they are relevant. Whether or not they may be available here on Guantanamo, is a second decision to be made, but only if I decide they are relevant. I have heard your arguments. I noted them. However, my ruling stands.

PRESIDENT: The Recorder has no witnesses, is that my understanding?

RECORDER: No, sir.

PRESIDENT: And there are no other approved witnesses to taken up. Ah, we will take a brief moment to review the unclassified evidence that we received so far and then we will pick back up in the proceeding.

MEMBER: If I might ask a question real quick of the PR. This is the entire translation of the hand written notes?

PERSONAL
REPRESENTATIVE: Yeah. The hand written notes are the Detainee is on yellow.

MEMBER: Yes.

PERSONAL
REPRESENTATIVE: and, then the next set of notes, hand written notes, are the Linguist's translation and then the final hard copy printed that's, ah, that...

MEMBER: Type written.

PERSONAL
REPRESENTATIVE: Typed from Linguist's notes.

MEMBER: Type from Linguist's translations. Okay.

PRESIDENT: Khalid Sheikh Muhammad, I did not offer you an oath early because I was informed by the Personal Representative that you would be making some statement later on in these proceedings relevant to the truthfulness of your comments. So, if you would like to take an oath I would administer one to you but I did understand that you going to make a statement.

DETAINEE: In the final statement, I will explain why then.

PRESIDENT: Alright. Thank you. [Tribunal pauses to review D-a thru D-d]

MEMBER: Seen those.

TRANSLATOR: Sir.

PRESIDENT: Yes.

TRANSLATOR: He wanted me to translate a Koranic verse on the spot.

PRESIDENT: I will permit it.

TRANSLATOR: Thank you.

TRANSLATOR: Can I ask him for clarification?

PRESIDENT: Yes.

PRESIDENT: Do you need a few more moments, Translator?

TRANSLATOR: Yes, sir, about thirty seconds.

PRESIDENT: Go ahead and take your time.

TRANSLATOR: Would you me to read the English translation after he read Arabic verse or would like him to read it.

PRESIDENT: You want to save that for later?

TRANSLATOR: [Nods head]

PRESIDENT: Alright.

PRESIDENT: Let me take up a few things that have come up as based on my review of these documents that have been provided to us so far. D-d, appears to be a written statement regarding certain treatment that you claim to have received at the hands of agents of the United Stated government as you indicated from the time of your capture in 2003 up until before coming here to Guantanamo in September 2006.

PRESIDENT: Is that correct?

DETAINEE: Yes.

PRESIDENT: Alright.

PRESIDENT: Now, I haven't seen any statements in the evidence we receive so far that claim to come from you other than acknowledging whether you were or not the head of the Military Committee.   Were any statements that you made as the result of any of the treatment that you received during that time frame from 2003 to 2006? Did you make those statements because of the treatment you receive from these people?

DETAINEE: Statement for whom?

PRESIDENT: To any of these interrogators.

DETAINEE: CIA peoples.   Yes.   At the beginning when they transferred me [REDACTED].

PRESIDENT: What I'm trying to get at is any statement that you made was it because of this treatment, to use your word, you claim torture. Do you make any statements because of that?

TRANSLATOR: Sir, for clarification.

PRESIDENT:	Can you translate it?
TRANSLATOR:	I will translate in Arabic.
PRESIDENT:	Yes.
TRANSLATOR:	[Translating above]
DETAINEE:	I ah cannot remember now [REDACTED] I'm senior man. Many people they know me which I don't them. I ask him even if he knew George Bush. He said, yes I do. He don't know you that not means its false. [REDACTED]. I said yes or not. This I said.
PRESIDENT:	Alright, I understand.
PRESIDENT:	Is there anything you would like to correct, amend, modify or explain to us from what you said back then?
DETAINEE:	I want to just it is not related enemy combatant but I'm saying for you to be careful with people. That you have classified and unclassified facts. My opinion to be fair with people. Because when I say, I will not regret when I say I'm enemy combatant. I did or not I know there are other but there are many Detainees which you receive classified against them maybe, maybe not take away from me for many Detainees false witnesses. This only advice.
PRESIDENT:	So you are aware that other...
DETAINEE:	Yes.
PRESIDENT	People made false statement as a result of this?
DETAINEE:	I did also.
PRESIDENT:	Uh huh.
DETAINEE:	I told him, I know him yes. There are and they are. Not even you show me. This I don't know him I never met him at all. So, unclassified which is both classified and unclassified so this is you know him you don't know him. You have to be fair with people. There are many many people which they have never been part of the Taliban. Afghanistan there have been many people arrested for example people who have been arrested after October 2001 after make attack against Afghanistan many of them just arrive after they don't what has happen. When Russian came to Afghanistan they felt they went back but they did anything with Taliban and al Qaida then came after that. I don't know why it was younger

ISN #10024
Enclosure (3)
Page 15 of 26

people same thing for Afghanis people they show Afghanis people. I will give example one. His name is Sayed Habib. This I remember. [REDACTED]

PRESIDENT: Alright.

PRESIDENT: Now what.

DETAINEE: For me nothing which was recorded. For which is written here is not related

PRESIDENT: I understand.

PRESIDENT: I do note that in one of the exhibits you indicate you are not under any pressure or duress today. Is that correct?

DETAINEE: That is about I'm hearing today. Yes.

PRESIDENT: So anything.

DETAINEE: Some of this information, I not state it to them.

PRESIDENT: The information that you are telling us today, so we are clear. You do not believe you are under any pressure or threat or duress to speak to us today, is that correct?

DETAINEE: Yes, that's correct.

PRESIDENT: Alright.

PRESIDENT: Now what you have told us about your previous treatment is on the record of these proceeding now and will be reported for any investigation that may be appropriate. Also, we will consider what you have told us in making our determination regarding your enemy combatant status.

DETAINEE: I hope you will take care of other Detainees with what I said. It's up to you.

PRESIDENT: I will do as I've said. I'll see to it that it is reported.

PRESIDENT: Alright. At this point, we are going to go into the final statement but I do want to give the opportunity to the Recorder, PR, and Tribunal member to ask questions if they would like. So, what will do is proceed then to the Detainee's final statement and then I'll have a question and answer session following that. Alright just give me a moment.

PRESIDENT: Alright.

PRESIDENT: Khalid Sheikh Muhammad, this concludes the presentation of unclassified information to the Tribunal. We are about to conclude the unclassified portion of the hearing. Do you wish to now make any final statement to the Tribunal? You have the assistance of your PR.

DETAINEE: I make a two part. Maybe he will read then I will go also.

PRESIDENT: Very well. You may continue.

PERSONAL

REPRESENTATIVE: Mr. President, the Detainee has asked me to read his final statement to the Tribunal with the understanding he may interject or add statements if he needs to, to correct what I say. According to the Detainee:

"I hereby admit and affirm without duress to the following:

1. I swore Bay'aat (i.e., allegiance) to Sheikh Usama Bin Laden to conduct Jihad of self and money, and also Hijrah (i.e., expatriation to any location in the world where Jihad is required).
2. I was a member of the Al Qaida Council.
3. I was the Media Operations Director for Al-Sahab, or 'The Clouds,' under Dr. Ayman Al-Zawahiri. Al-Sahab is the media outlet that provided Al-Qaida-sponsored information to Al Jazeera. Four. "

DETAINEE: [speaking inaudibly to Personal Representative]

PRESIDENT: Please tell.

PERSONAL
REPRESENTATIVE: In other channels or other media outlets.

PRESIDENT: Thank you.

PERSONAL
REPRESENTATIVE: [continuing] "4. I was the Operational Director for Sheikh Usama Bin Laden for the organizing, planning, follow-up, and execution of the 9/11 Operation under the Military Commander, Sheikh Abu Hafs Al-Masri Subhi Abu Sittah.
5. I was the Military Operational Commander for all foreign operations around the world under the direction of Sheikh Usama Bin Laden and Dr. Ayman Al-Zawahiri.
6. I was directly in charge, after the death of Sheikh Abu Hafs Al-Masri Subhi Abu Sittah, of managing and following up on the Cell for the Production of Biological Weapons, such as anthrax and others, and following up on Dirty Bomb Operations on American soil.
7. I was Emir (i.e., commander) of Beit Al Shuhada (i.e., the Martyrs' House) in the state of Kandahar, Afghanistan, which housed the 9/11 hijackers. There I was responsible for their

training and readiness for the execution of the 9/11 Operation. Also, I hereby admit and affirm without duress that I was a responsible participant, principal planner, trainer, financier (via the Military Council Treasury), executor, and/or a personal participant in the following:

1. I was responsible for the 1993 World Trade Center Operation.
2. I was responsible for the 9/11 Operation, from A to Z.
3. I decapitated with my blessed right hand the head of the American Jew, Daniel Pearl, in the city of Karachi, Pakistan. For those who would like to confirm, there are pictures of me on the Internet holding his head.
4. I was responsible for the Shoe Bomber Operation to down two American airplanes.
5. I was responsible for the Filka Island Operation in Kuwait that killed two American soldiers.
6. I was responsible for the bombing of a nightclub in Bali, Indonesia, which was frequented by British and Australian nationals.
7. I was responsible for planning, training, surveying, and financing the New (or Second) Wave attacks against the following skyscrapers after 9/11:
   a. Library Tower, California.
   b. Sears Tower, Chicago,
   c. Plaza Bank, Washington state.
   d. The Empire State Building, New York City.
8. I was responsible for planning, financing, & follow-up of Operations to destroy American military vessels and oil tankers in the Straights of Hormuz, the Straights of Gibralter, and the Port of Singapore.
9. I was responsible for planning, training, surveying, and financing for the Operation to bomb and destroy the Panama Canal.
10. I was responsible for surveying and financing for the assassination of several former American Presidents, including President Carter.
11. I was responsible for surveying, planning, and financing for the bombing of suspension bridges in New York.
12. I was responsible for planning to destroy the Sears Tower by burning a few fuel or oil tanker trucks beneath it or around it.
13. I was responsible for planning, surveying, and financing for the operation to destroy Heathrow Airport, the Canary Wharf Building, and Big Ben on British soil.
14. I was responsible for planning, surveying, and financing for the destruction of many night clubs frequented by American and British citizens on Thailand soil.
15. I was responsible for surveying and financing for the destruction of the New York Stock Exchange and other financial targets after 9/11.
16. I was responsible for planning, financing, and surveying for the destruction of buildings in the Israeli city of Elat by using airplanes leaving from Saudi Arabia.
17. I was responsible for planning, surveying, and financing for the destruction of American embassies in Indonesia, Australia, and Japan.

18. I was responsible for surveying and financing for the destruction of the Israeli embassy in India, Azerbaijan, the Philippines, and Australia.
19. I was responsible for surveying and financing for the destruction of an Israeli 'El-Al' Airlines flight on Thailand soil departing from Bangkok Airport.
20. I was responsible for sending several Mujahadeen into Israel to conduct surveillance to hit several strategic targets deep in Israel.
21. I was responsible for the bombing of the hotel in Mombasa that is frequented by Jewish travelers via El-Al airlines.
22. I was responsible for launching a Russian-made SA-7 surface-to-air missile on El-Al or other Jewish airliner departing from Mombasa.
23. I was responsible for planning and surveying to hit American targets in South Korea, such as American military bases and a few night clubs frequented by American soldiers.
24. I was responsible for financial, excuse me, I was responsible for providing financial support to hit American, Jewish, and British targets in Turkey.
25. I was responsible for surveillance needed to hit nuclear power plants that generate electricity in several U.S. states.
26. I was responsible for planning, surveying, and financing to hit NATO Headquarters in Europe.
27. I was responsible for the planning and surveying needed to execute the Bojinka Operation, which was designed to down twelve American airplanes full of passengers. I personally monitored a round-trip, Manila-to-Seoul, Pan Am flight.
28. I was responsible for the assassination attempt against President Clinton during his visit to the Philippines in 1994 or 1995.
29. I was responsible for the assassination attempt against Pope John Paul the second while he was visiting the Philippines."

DETAINEE: I was not responsible, but share.

PERSONAL
REPRESENTATIVE: I shared responsibility. I will restate number twenty nine.

29. "I shared responsibility for the assassination attempt against Pope John Paul the second while he was visiting the Philippines.

30. I was responsible for the training and financing for the assassination of Pakistan's President Musharaf.

31. I was responsible for the attempt to destroy an American oil company owned by the Jewish former Secretary of State, Henry Kissinger, on the Island of Sumatra, Indonesia."

PERSONAL
REPRESENTATIVE: Sir, that concludes the written portion of the Detainee's final statement and as he has alluded to earlier he has some additional comments he would like to make.

PRESIDENT: Alright. Before you proceed, Khalid Sheikh Muhammad, the statement that was just read by the Personal Representative, were those your words?

BEGIN DETAINEE ORAL STATEMENT

DETAINEE: Yes. And I want to add some of this one just for some verification. It like some operations before I join al Qaida. Before I remember al Qaida which is related to *Bojinka Operation* I went to destination involve to us in 94, 95. Some Operations which means out of al Qaida. It's like beheading Daniel Pearl. It's not related to al Qaida. It was shared in Pakistani. Other group, Mujahadeen. The story of Daniel Pearl, because he stated for the Pakistanis, group that he was working with the both. His mission was in Pakistan to track about Richard Reed trip to Israel. Richard Reed, do you have trip? You send it Israel to make set for targets in Israel. His mission in Pakistan from Israeli intelligence, Mosad, to make interview to ask about when he was there. Also, he mention to them he was both. He have relation with CIA people and were the Mosad. But he was not related to al Qaida at all or UBL. It is related to the Pakistan Mujahadeen group. Other operations mostly are some word I'm not accurate in saying. I'm responsible but if you read the heading history. The line there [Indicating to Personal Representative a place or Exhibit D-c].

PERSONAL
REPRESENTATIVE: [Reading] "Also, hereby admit and affirm without duress that I was a responsible participant, principle planner, trainer, financier."

DETAINEE: For this is not necessary as I responsible, responsible. But with in these things responsible participant in finances.

PRESIDENT: I understand. I want to be clear, though, is you that were the author of that document.

DETAINEE: That's right.

PRESIDENT: That it is true?

DETAINEE: That's true.

PRESIDENT: Alright. You may continue with your statement.

DETAINEE: Okay. I start in Arabic.

PRESIDENT: Please.

DETAINEE
(through translator): In the name of God the most compassionate, the most merciful, and if any fail to retaliation by way of charity and. I apologize. I will start again. And if any fail to judge by the light of Allah has revealed, they are no better than wrong doers, unbelievers, and the unjust.

DETAINEE: For this verse, I not take the oath. Take an oath is a part of your Tribunal and I'll not accept it. To be or accept the Tribunal as to be, I'll accept it. That I'm accepting American constitution, American law or whatever you are doing here. This is why religiously I cannot accept anything you do. Just to explain for this one, does not mean I'm not saying that I'm lying. When I not take oath does not mean I'm lying. You know very well peoples take oath and they will lie. You know the President he did this before he just makes his oath and he lied. So sometimes when I'm not making oath does not mean I'm lying.

PRESIDENT: I understand.

DETAINEE: Second thing. When I wrote this thing, I mean, the PR he told me that President may stop you at anytime and he don't like big mouth nor you to talk too much. To be within subject. So, I will try to be within the enemy combatant subject

PRESIDENT: You can say whatever you'd like to say so long as it's relevant to what we are discussing here today.

DETAINEE: Okay, thanks.

DETAINEE: What I wrote here, is not I'm making myself hero, when I said I was responsible for this or that. But your are military man. You know very well there are language for any war. So, there are, we are when I admitting these things I'm not saying I'm not did it. I did it but this the language of any war. If America they want to invade Iraq they will not send for Saddam roses or kisses they send for a bombardment. This is the best way if I want. If I'm fighting for anybody admit to them I'm American enemies. For sure, I'm American enemies. Usama bin Laden, he did his best press conference in American media. Mr. John Miller he been there when he made declaration against Jihad, against America. And he said it is not no need for me now to make explanation of what he said but mostly he said about American military presence in Arabian peninsula and aiding Israel and many things. So when we made any war against America we are jackals fighting in the nights. I consider myself, for what you are doing, a religious thing as you

ISN #10024
Enclosure (3)
Page 21 of 26

consider us fundamentalist. So, we derive from religious leading that we consider we and George Washington doing same thing. As consider George Washington as hero. Muslims many of them are considering Usama bin Laden. He is doing same thing. He is just fighting. He needs his independence. Even we think that, or not me only. Many Muslims, that al Qaida or Taliban they are doing. They have been oppressed by America. This is the feeling of the prophet. So when we say we are enemy combatant, that right. We are. But I'm asking you again to be fair with many Detainees which are not enemy combatant. Because many of them have been unjustly arrested. Many, not one or two or three. Cause the definition you which wrote even from my view it is not fair. Because if I was in the first Jihad times Russia. So I have to be Russian enemy. But America supported me in this because I'm their alliances when I was fighting Russia. Same job I'm doing. I'm fighting. I was fighting there Russia now I'm fighting America. So, many people who been in Afghanistan never live. Afghanistan stay in but they not share Taliban or al Qaida. They been Russian time and they cannot go back to their home with their corrupted government. They stayed there and when America invaded Afghanistan parliament. They had been arrest. They never have been with Taliban or the others. So many people consider them as enemy but they are not. Because definitions are very wide definition so people they came after October of 2002, 2001. When America invaded Afghanistan, they just arrive in Afghanistan cause the hear there enemy. They don't know what it means al Qaida or Usama bin Laden or Taliban. They don't care about these things. They heard they were enemy in Afghanistan they just arrived. As they heard first time Russian invade Afghanistan. They arrive they fought when back than they came. They don't know what's going on and Taliban they been head of government. You consider me even Taliban even the president of whole government. Many people they join Taliban because they are the government. When Karzai they came they join Karzai when come they join whatever public they don't know what is going on. So, many Taliban fight even the be fighters because they just because public. The government is Taliban then until now CIA don't have exactly definition well who is Taliban, who is al Qaida. Your Tribunal now are discussing he is enemy or not and that is one of your jobs. So this is why you find many Afghanis people, Pakistanis people even, they don't know what going on they just hear they are fighting and they help Muslim in Afghanistan. Then what. There are some infidels which they came here and they have to help them. But then there weren't any intend to do anything against America. Taliban themselves between Taliban they said Afghanistan which they never again against 9/11 operation. The rejection between senior of Taliban of what al Qaida are doing. Many of Taliban rejected what they are doing. Even many Taliban, they not agree about why we are in Afghanistan. Some of them they have been with us. Taliban never in their life at all before America invade them the intend to do anything against America. They never been with al Qaida. Does not mean we are here as American now. They gave political asylum for many countries. They gave for Chinese oppositions or a North Korean but that does not mean they are with them same thing many of Taliban. They harbor us as al Qaida does not mean we are together. So, this is why I'm asking you to be fair with Afghanis and Pakistanis and many Arabs which been in Afghanistan. Many of them been unjustly. The funny story they been Sunni government they sent some spies to assassinate UBL then we arrested them sent them to Afghanistan/Taliban. Taliban put them into prison. Americans they came and arrest them as enemy combatant. They brought them here. So, even if they are my enemy but not fair to be there with me. This is what I'm saying. The way of the war, you know, very well, any country waging war against their enemy the language of the war are killing. If man and woman they be together as a marriage that is up to the kids, children. But if you and me, two nations, will be together in war the others are victims. This is the way of the language. You know 40 million people were killed in World War One. Ten million kill in World War. You know that two million four hundred thousand be killed in the Korean War. So this language of the war. Any people who, when Usama bin Laden say I'm waging war because such such reason, now he declared it. But when you said I'm terrorist, I think it is deceiving peoples. Terrorists, enemy combatant. All these definitions as CIA you can make whatever you want. Now, you told me when I ask about the witnesses, I'm not convinced that this related to the matter. It is up to you. Maybe I'm convinced but your are head and he [gesturing to Personal Representative] is not responsible, the other, because your are head of the committee. So, finally it's your war but the problem is no definitions of many words. It would be widely definite that many people be oppressed. Because war, for sure, there will be victims. When I said I'm not happy that three thousand been killed in America. I feel sorry even. I don't like to kill children and the kids. Never Islam are, give me green light to kill peoples. Killing, as in the Christianity, Jews, and Islam, are prohibited. But there are exception of rule when you are killing people in Iraq. You said we have to do it. We don't like Saddam. But this is the way to deal with Saddam. Same thing you are saying. Same language you use, I use. When you are invading two- thirds of Mexican, you call your war manifest destiny. It up to you to call it what you want. But other side are calling you oppressors. If now George Washington. If now we were living in the Revolutionary War and George Washington he being arrested through Britain. For sure he, they would consider him enemy combatant. But American they consider him as hero. This right the any Revolutionary War they will be as George Washington or Britain. So we are considered American Army bases which we have from seventies in Iraq. Also, in the Saudi Arabian, Kuwait, Qatar, and Bahrain. This is kind of invasion, but I'm not here to convince you. Is not or not but mostly speech is ask you to be fair with people. I'm don't have anything to say that I'm not enemy. This is why the language of any war in the world is killing. I mean the language of the war is victims. I don't like to kill people. I feel very sorry they been killed kids in 9/11. What I will do? This is the language. Sometime I want to make great awakening between American to stop foreign policy in our land. I know American people are torturing us from seventies. [REDACTED] I know they talking about human rights. And I know it is against American Constitution, against American laws. But they said every law, they have exceptions, this is your bad luck you been part of the exception of our laws. They got have something to convince me but we are doing same language. But we are saying we have Sharia law, but we have Koran. What is enemy combatant in my language?

DETAINEE
(through translator): Allah forbids you not with regards to those who fight you not for your faith nor drive you out of your homes from dealing kindly and justly with them. For Allah love those who are just. There is one more sentence. Allah only forbids you with regards to those who fight you for your faith and drive you out of your homes and support others in driving you out from turning to them for friendship and protection. It is such as turn to them in these circumstances that do wrong.

DETAINEE: So we are driving from whatever deed we do we ask about Koran or Hadith. We are not making up for us laws. When we need Fatwa from the religious we have to go back to see what they said scholar. To see what they said yes or not. Killing is prohibited in all what you call the people of the book, Jews, Judaism, Christianity, and Islam. You know the Ten Commandments very well. The Ten Commandments are shared between all of us. We all are serving one God. Then now kill you know it very well. But war language also we have language for the war. You have to kill. But you have to care if unintentionally or intentionally target if I have if I'm not at the Pentagon. I consider it is okay. If I target now when we target in USA we choose them military target, economical, and political. So, war central victims mostly means economical target. So if now American they know UBL. He is in this house they don't care about his kids and his. They will just bombard it. They will kill all of them and they did it. They kill wife of Dr. Ayman Zawahiri and his two daughters and his son in one bombardment. They receive a report that is his house be. He had not been there. They killed them. They arrested my kids intentionally. They are kids. They been arrested for four months they had been abused. So, for me I have patience. I know I'm not talk about what's come to me. The American have human right. So, enemy combatant itself, it flexible word. So I think God knows that many who been arrested, they been unjustly arrested. Otherwise, military throughout history know very well. They don't war will never stop. War start from Adam when Cain he killed Abel until now. It's never gonna stop killing of people. This is the

UNCLASSIFIED

way of the language. American start the Revolutionary War then they starts the Mexican then Spanish War then World War One, World War Two. You read the history. You know never stopping war. This is life. But if who is enemy combatant and who is not? Finally, I finish statement. I'm asking you to be fair with other people.

PRESIDENT: Does that conclude your statement, Khalid Sheikh Muhammad?

DETAINEE: Yes.

PRESIDENT: Alright.

DETAINEE QUESTION & ANSWER

PRESIDENT: Does the Personal Representative have any questions for the Detainee based on his statement?

PERSONAL
REPRESENTATIVE: No, Sir.

PRESIDENT: Does the Recorder have any questions for the Detainee?

RECORDER: No, Sir.

PRESIDENT: Do either of the Tribunal members wish to question the Detainee?

MEMBERS: No, sir. Nothing further Sir.

PRESIDENT: Alright.

CLOSING UNCLASSIFIED SESSION

PRESIDENT: All unclassified evidence having been provided to the Tribunal, this concludes the open tribunal session.

PRESIDENT: Khalid Sheikh Muhammad, you shall be notified of the Tribunal decision upon completion of the review of these proceed by the Combatant Status Review Tribunal convening authority in Washington, D.C. If, the Tribunal determines that you should not be classified as an enemy combatant, you will be released to your home country as soon as arrangements can be made. If however, the Tribunal determines your classification as an enemy combatant you may be eligible for an Administrative Review Board hearing at a future date.

UNCLASSIFIED

PRESIDENT: The Administrative Review Board will make an assessment of whether there is continued reason to believe that you pose a threat to the United States or its coalition partners in the ongoing armed conflict against terrorist organizations such as al Qaeda and its affiliates and supporters or whether there are other factors bearing upon the need for continued detention.

PRESIDENT: You will have the opportunity to be heard and to present relevant information to the Administrative Review Board. You can present information from your family and friends that might help you at that Board. You are encouraged to contact them as soon as possible to begin to gather information that may help you.

PRESIDENT: A military officer will be assigned at a later date to assist you in the Administrative Review Board process.

ADJOURN OPEN SESSION

PRESIDENT: The open session of this Tribunal hearing is adjourned.

RECORDER: The time is 2:43pm. The date is 10 March 2007.

RECORDER: All Rise.

[The Tribunal withdrew from the hearing room]

AUTHENTICATION

I certify the material contained in this transcript is a true and accurate verbatim rendering of the testimony and English language translation of Detainee's words given during the open session of the Combatant Status Review Tribunal of ISN 10024.

[REDATED]
CAPT JAGC USN
Tribunal President

www.ingramcontent.com/pod-product-compliance
Lightning Source LLC
Chambersburg PA
CBHW080805290526
45790CB00008B/3590